WHEN I'M ON MY KNEES
Prayer Journal

from the best-selling
devotional by
ANITA CORRINE DONIHUE

BARBOUR
PUBLISHING, INC.
Uhrichsville, Ohio

Scripture quotations marked KJV are taken from the King James Version of the Bible.

Scripture quotations marked NIV are taken from the HOLY BIBLE: NEW INTERNATIONAL VERSION. ® NIV. ® Copyright © 1973, 1978, 1984 by International Bible Society. Used by permission of Zondervan Publishing House. All rights reserved.

Published by Barbour Publishing, Inc., P.O. Box 719, Uhrichsville, Ohio 44683 http://www.barbourbooks.com

Member of the
Evangelical Christian
Publishers Association

Printed in the United States of America.

Introduction

With well over 300,000 copies sold, the bestselling book *When I'm on My Knees* has become a modern devotional classic. Author Anita Corrine Donihue's gentle writing style—full of spiritual joy, affirmation, encouragement, and challenge—speaks to women of all ages, walks of life, and circumstances.

When I'm on My Knees Prayer Journal is the perfect companion to the original devotional book. Each page features a brief selection from *When I'm on My Knees* or a selected Bible verse, followed by lined space for your own journaling. Use this book to record prayer requests or praise notes, Bible study insights, or what God is teaching you through your daily experiences.

Take a few minutes each day to make a record of your spiritual journey, and say along with Anita Donihue:

> *Father, here are my concerns and needs. I commit them to You. I thank You in Jesus' name for the answers that will come according to Your will. I trust Your wisdom and give You all the praise.*

$\mathcal{W}$ell, all we can do is pray about it."

Oh, no! I can't believe I said that. Again. All we can do is pray? How shortsighted can I be? Great things happen while I'm on my knees.

*F*orces of
heaven are released
when one person
goes to prayer.

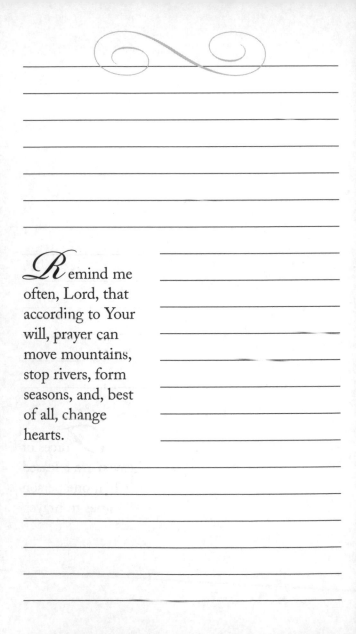

$\mathcal{R}$emind me often, Lord, that according to Your will, prayer can move mountains, stop rivers, form seasons, and, best of all, change hearts.

And he who searches our hearts knows the mind of the Spirit, because the Spirit intercedes for the saints in accordance with God's will.

PHILIPPIANS 4:27 KJV

*F*ather, thank You for being so patient with me. For the many times I mess things up and You are still there for me, I am grateful.

You protect me from harm's way, wrapping Your wings about me as an eagle protects her young. She carries them on her wings and doesn't let them fall. Thank You for carrying me, too.

I marvel that You know me so well. You know the hairs on my head. You care about the pain in my head, my hands, my back, my feet. When a sparrow falls, You care. How much then You must care for me.

B less the Lord, O my soul: and all that is within me, bless his holy name. Bless the Lord, O my soul, and forget not all his benefits.

PSALM 103:1–2 KJV

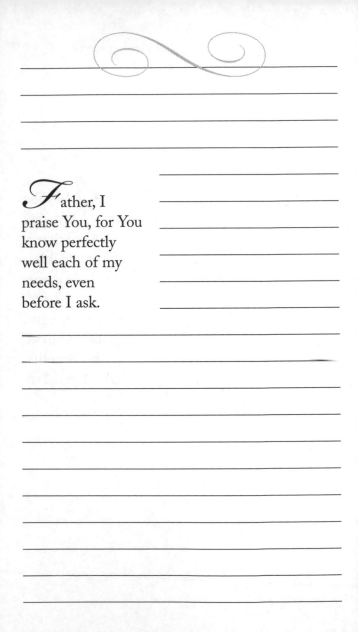

*F*ather, I
praise You, for You
know perfectly
well each of my
needs, even
before I ask.

*T*hank You, Lord, for being my Shepherd. Thank You for watching over and protecting me as a shepherd does his sheep.

I feel confident and unafraid as You direct me each day. When You provide for me, I find enough overflowing goodness to share with others.

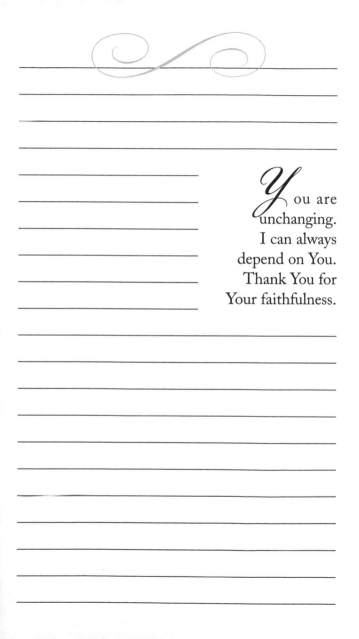

*Y*ou are
unchanging.
I can always
depend on You.
Thank You for
Your faithfulness.

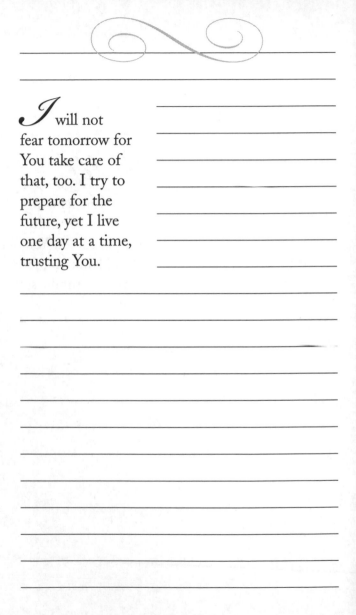

$\mathcal{I}$ will not fear tomorrow for You take care of that, too. I try to prepare for the future, yet I live one day at a time, trusting You.

*S*ing to the Lord a new song; sing to the Lord, all the earth. Sing to the Lord, praise his name; proclaim his salvation day after day.

PSALM 96:1–2 NIV

I shudder at how I was once in sin's bondage, Lord Jesus. Then You saved me. All I had to do was ask You into my heart, and You forgave my every single sin.

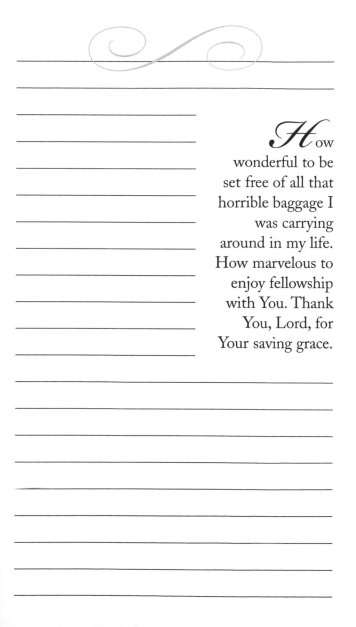

*H*ow wonderful to be set free of all that horrible baggage I was carrying around in my life. How marvelous to enjoy fellowship with You. Thank You, Lord, for Your saving grace.

*H*ere in calm communion I seek Your guidance. Thank You for how You lead me along the right paths.

*N*o longer
will I depend on
my own good
works, but instead
on Your wonderful
grace. Thanks be
to You, God!

*I*f thou, Lord, shouldest mark iniquities, O Lord, who shall stand?

But there is forgiveness with thee, that thou mayest be feared.

I wait for the Lord, my soul doth wait, and in his word do I hope.

PSALM 130:3–5 KJV

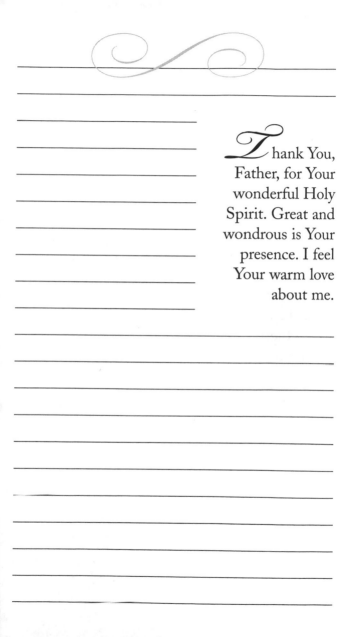

Thank You, Father, for Your wonderful Holy Spirit. Great and wondrous is Your presence. I feel Your warm love about me.

*H*oly Spirit, fill me daily. Groom me so I may produce the fruits of Your Spirit. Make my cup overflow so I may be a blessing to those around me.

*B*ut the fruit of the Spirit is love, joy, peace, patience, kindness, goodness, faithfulness, gentleness, and self-control. Against such things there is no law.

GALATIANS 5:22–23 NIV

You are my joy and my strength. I will not fear. Instead, I will unceasingly sing Your praises.

*S*ing to the
Lord a new song,
his praise from the
ends of the earth.
ISAIAH 42:10 NIV

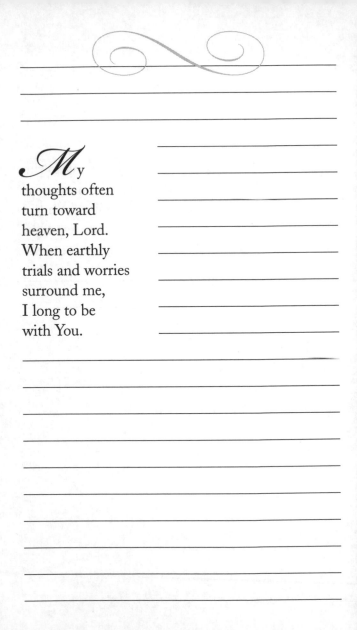

*M*y thoughts often turn toward heaven, Lord. When earthly trials and worries surround me, I long to be with You.

*A*ll the money I could earn, the treasure I can obtain, the land I may plan to buy are nothing in light of my eternal home with You.

*E*arthly things lose their value. They wear out, rust, fade, and are sometimes stolen. The eternal treasures I store in heaven with You can never be taken from me.

I'll invest my meager riches in You and Your work. I can't help but love You more than anything the world can give me.

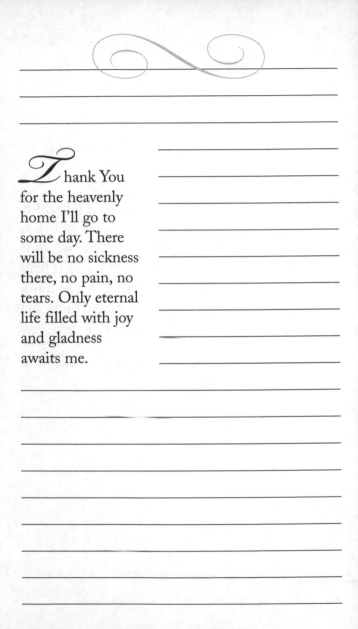

$\mathcal{T}$hank You
for the heavenly
home I'll go to
some day. There
will be no sickness
there, no pain, no
tears. Only eternal
life filled with joy
and gladness
awaits me.

*H*e will wipe every tear from their eyes. There will be no more death or mourning or crying or pain, for the old order of things has passed away.

REVELATION 21:4 NIV

*L*ord,
thank You for my
country and the
freedoms we have.

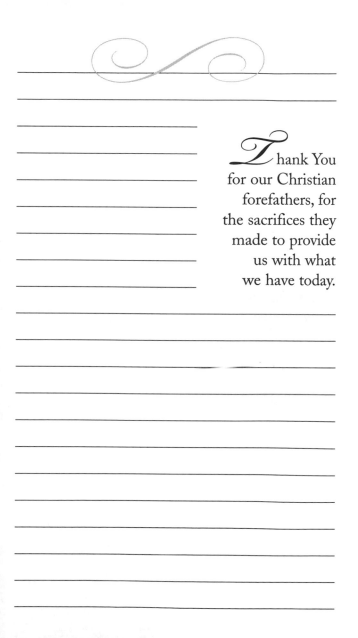

*T*hank You for our Christian forefathers, for the sacrifices they made to provide us with what we have today.

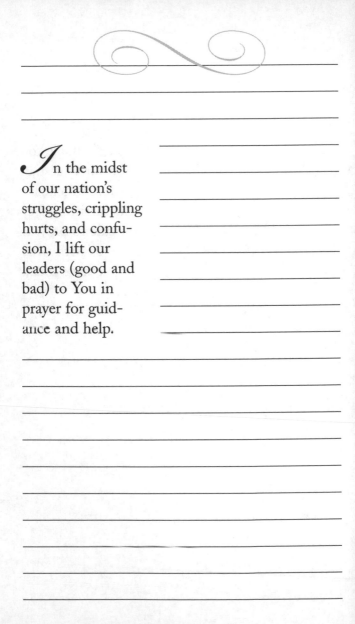

*I*n the midst of our nation's struggles, crippling hurts, and confusion, I lift our leaders (good and bad) to You in prayer for guidance and help.

$\mathcal{R}$evive us
spiritually. May
we regain the
standards we have
so carelessly
thrown away
and once again
become one nation
under God.

*C*leanse our sins and heal our land, I pray. Deliver us from drugs and violence. Help our people who love You to step forth and speak out for what is right.

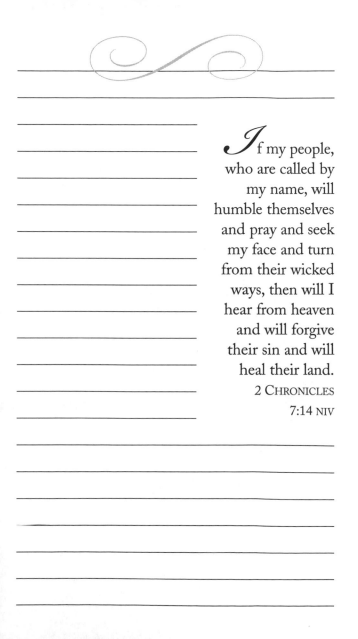

*I*f my people, who are called by my name, will humble themselves and pray and seek my face and turn from their wicked ways, then will I hear from heaven and will forgive their sin and will heal their land.

2 CHRONICLES 7:14 NIV

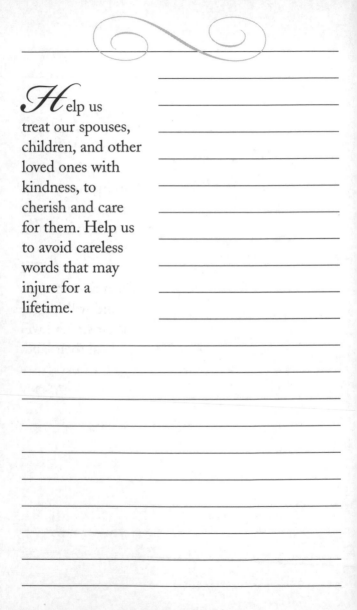

$\mathcal{H}$elp us
treat our spouses,
children, and other
loved ones with
kindness, to
cherish and care
for them. Help us
to avoid careless
words that may
injure for a
lifetime.

*L*ord, we know we cannot have strong family units without following Your teachings. You know our hearts. Let our lives please You.

$\mathcal{T}$oday was
one of those days,
Lord, where
everything seemed
to go wrong.
There were many
anxious moments.
All of a sudden I
felt calm. Was
someone praying
for me?

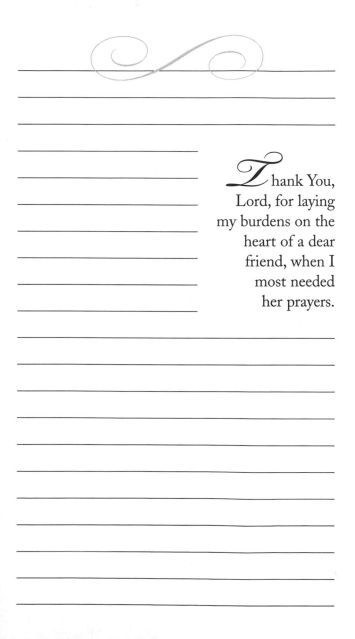

Thank You, Lord, for laying my burdens on the heart of a dear friend, when I most needed her prayers.

Another chaotic day. Responsibilities—schedules—deadlines. Then I feel Your nudge. I recognize Your voice.

*S*omeone comes to mind. I realize the need to pray. Now! I may not even know why. The world stops around me. I offer silent prayer.

*Y*ou bring
the prayer
need to mind
repeatedly
throughout
the day. I
keep praying.

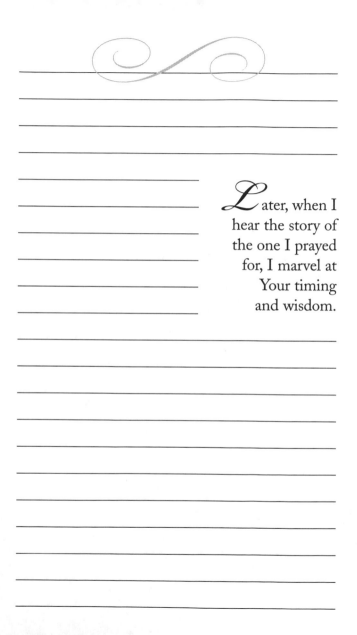

*L*ater, when I
hear the story of
the one I prayed
for, I marvel at
Your timing
and wisdom.

I can't change
others, only
myself.

*T*hank You for helping me see the good in people, the best in difficult situations. Thank You for teaching me to recall the good events in life and help me not to dwell on the bad ones.

*T*hank You for my Bible, Your Word. How dear it is to me. Each day I draw nourishment and direction from it. How rich its words are!

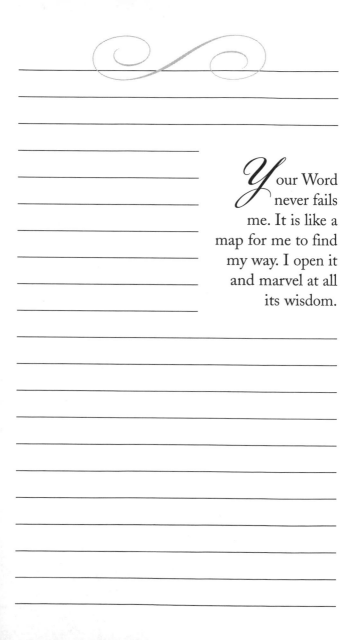

*Y*our Word never fails me. It is like a map for me to find my way. I open it and marvel at all its wisdom.

$\mathcal{P}$raise You,
dear Lord. Teach
me Your countless
lessons. I will
repeat them on my
lips and hide them
in my heart as You
have shown me. I
will rejoice in all I
learn. I will medi-
tate on Your Word
and praise You
through my nights
and days.

I have hidden
your word in
my heart that I
might not sin
against you.
PSALM 119:11 NIV

I wake in the hush of night with dawn lacing together shadows and shimmers, silhouetted by a silvery moon. I slip outside and listen to the silence. Might I hear Your voice?

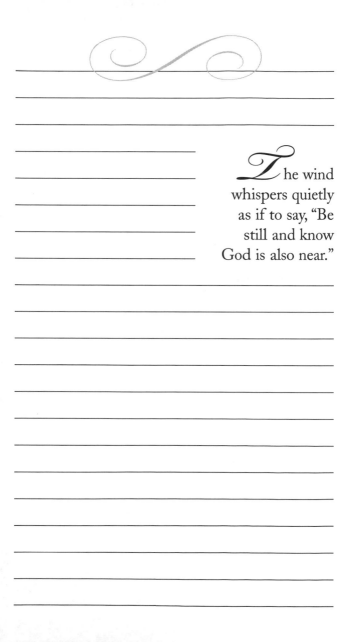

*T*he wind
whispers quietly
as if to say, "Be
still and know
God is also near."

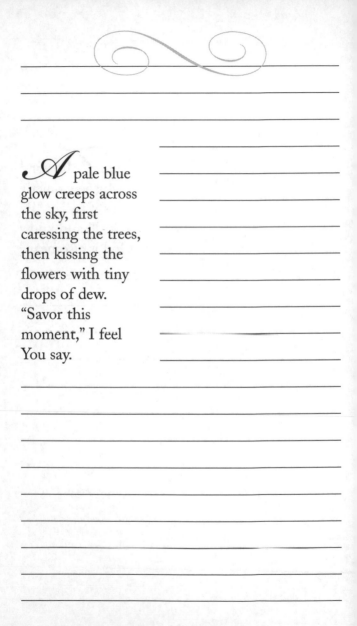

A pale blue glow creeps across the sky, first caressing the trees, then kissing the flowers with tiny drops of dew. "Savor this moment," I feel You say.

$\mathcal{C}$ arry the strength I give into your busy, strenuous day. My Spirit goes with you. Take time today to bless others."

Ah, yes, Lord, I will.

*T*hank You,
Lord, for Your
wondrous works
and all the things
You do for me. I
praise You with
my whole heart
and soul.

So many times You shower Your mercy on me and forgive my sins. You reach down and heal my tired body. Your love, mercy, and patience go beyond measure.

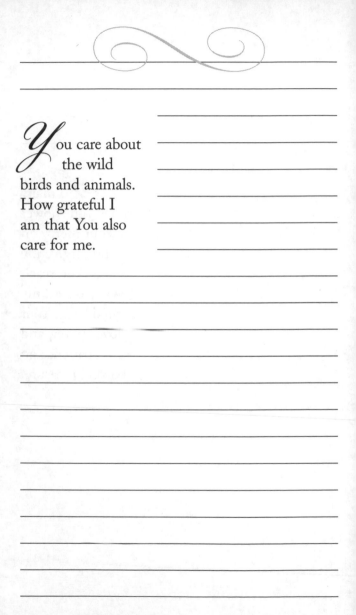

*Y*ou care about the wild birds and animals. How grateful I am that You also care for me.

O Lord, how
manifold are
thy works! In
wisdom hast thou
made them all:
the earth is full
of thy riches.
PSALM 104:24 KJV

You created my inner-most being and molded me in my mother's womb. You knew the color of my hair and eyes and the shape of my nose before I was ever born, so now I thank You for them.

I'm glad I'm me, and I'm thankful that You made me. I want to be a blessing for You—just the way I am.

*I*f my accomplishments should go unrecognized, no matter. I feel good about them. Best of all, I know You are proud of me and that You love me.

I am the vine, ye are the branches: He that abideth in me, and I in him, the same bringeth forth much fruit: for without me ye can do nothing.

JOHN 15:5 KJV

$\mathscr{F}$orgive and
you will be
forgiven."
LUKE 6:37 NIV

*H*as it been seventy times seven that I have forgiven? Help me show gentleness and forgiveness as You do.

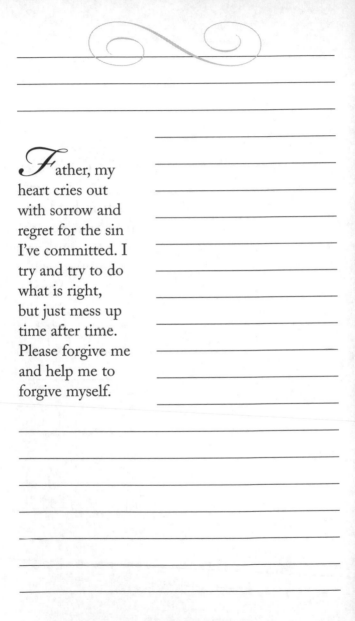

$\mathcal{F}$ather, my heart cries out with sorrow and regret for the sin I've committed. I try and try to do what is right, but just mess up time after time. Please forgive me and help me to forgive myself.

*M*y dear child, what other times? I've washed all that away with my blood. Forgive as I forgive you. Love, Jesus"

Dear Father, how can I pay these bills? I give it to You, dear Lord. I place myself and these bills in Your hands and ask for Your direction.

*S*how me how I can help others even while I hurt financially. Help me share a portion of my earnings with You for Your glory. Remind me to give You first place in my pocketbook!

$\mathcal{E}$nable me to trust You to provide for my needs so I won't worry about food or drink, money or clothes. You already know my needs. I thank You for providing.

$\mathcal{L}$et me not be anxious about tomorrow. I know You will take care of that, too. I will take each day as it comes and commit it to You.

Therefore I tell you, do not worry about your life, what you will eat or drink; or about your body, what you will wear."

MATTHEW 6:25 NIV

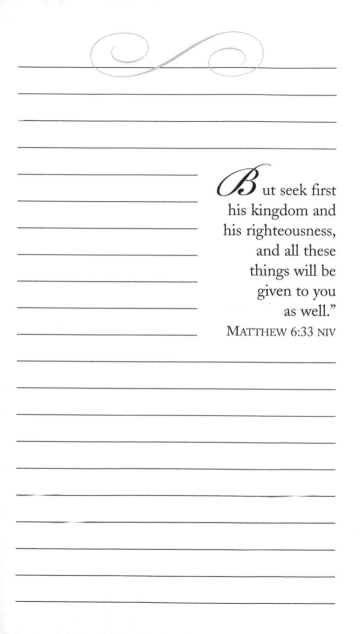

"$\mathcal{B}$ ut seek first his kingdom and his righteousness, and all these things will be given to you as well."

MATTHEW 6:33 NIV

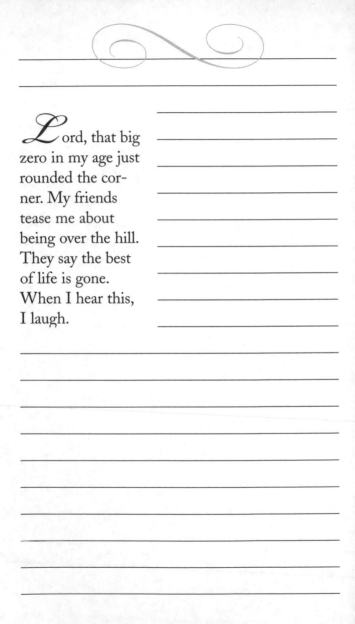

$\mathcal{L}$ord, that big zero in my age just rounded the corner. My friends tease me about being over the hill. They say the best of life is gone. When I hear this, I laugh.

I wonder what
You have in store
for me this next
year. How can You
use me during this
phase of my life? I
have no fear of
growing older.
Life is out there
to enjoy.

I may be growing older, but I refuse to grow and act old. Old age is an attitude. I'm determined to live life abundantly through Your joy and strength.

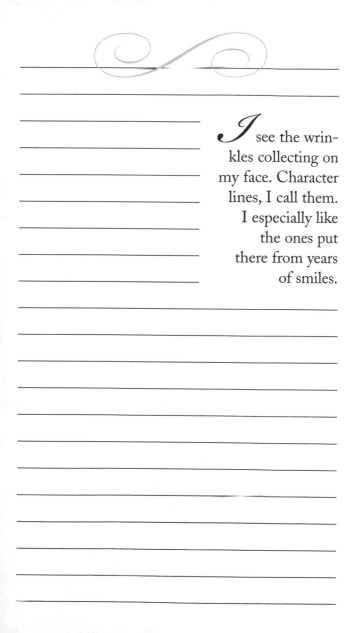

$\mathcal{I}$ see the wrinkles collecting on my face. Character lines, I call them. I especially like the ones put there from years of smiles.

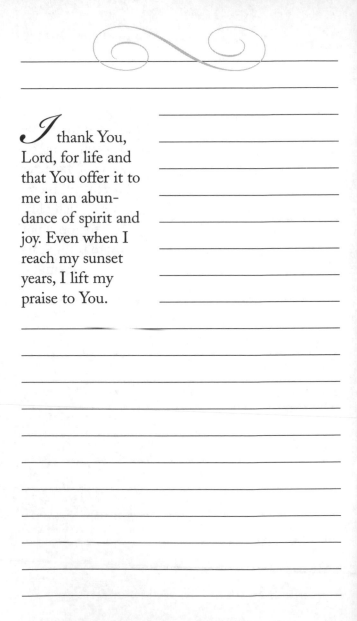

I thank You, Lord, for life and that You offer it to me in an abundance of spirit and joy. Even when I reach my sunset years, I lift my praise to You.

*F*avour is
deceitful, and
beauty is vain: but
a woman that
feareth the Lord,
she shall be
praised.

PROVERBS 31:30 KJV

*F*ather, I give You my heart, my soul, my life. I dedicate my whole being to You. I give You my failures and my successes, my fears and my aspirations.

*F*ill me with
Your spirit, I
pray; enable me to
do the tasks set
before me. Lead
me into Your ever-
lasting way.

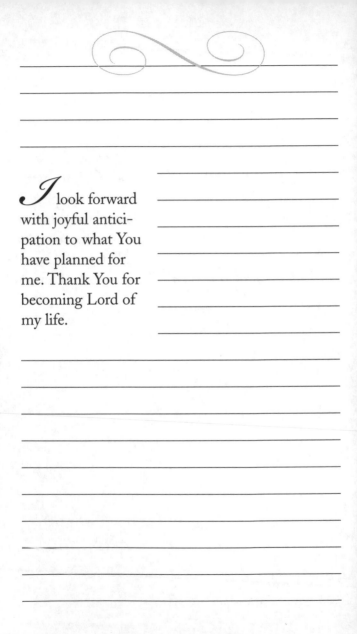

I look forward with joyful anticipation to what You have planned for me. Thank You for becoming Lord of my life.

Search me, O God, and know my heart; test me and know my anxious thoughts. See if there is any offensive way in me, and lead me in the way everlasting.

PSALM 139:23–24 NIV

$\mathcal{W}$e must remember God knows our future. He has our concerns and best interests at heart.

*A*long the way, we may not understand the reasoning of His direction for us. As we continue walking by faith in the paths He blazes, we'll learn His answers.

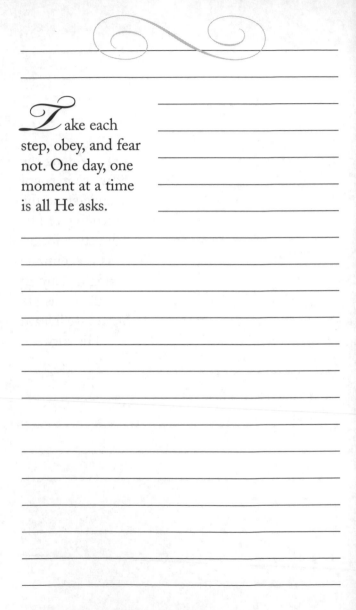

$\mathcal{T}$ake each step, obey, and fear not. One day, one moment at a time is all He asks.

*W*hen troubles come, look to Him, plant your feet on His path, and dig in your toes. Don't waver! He'll show the best way. He has already walked the path.

I take comfort
in Your presence
and cling to the
assurance that
You, the Rose
of Sharon, will
always abide
with me.

The grass withereth, the flower fadeth: but the word of our God shall stand forever.

ISAIAH 40:8 KJV

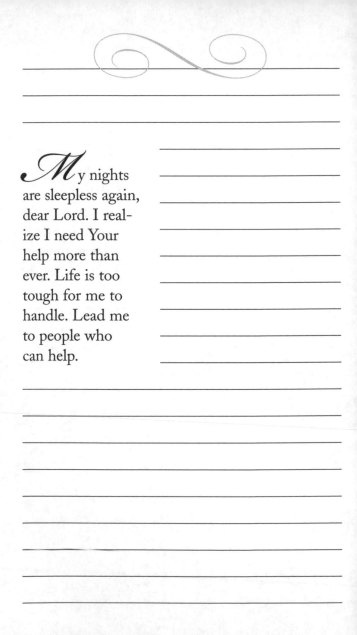

*M*y nights are sleepless again, dear Lord. I realize I need Your help more than ever. Life is too tough for me to handle. Lead me to people who can help.

*L*et me give
my burdens all to
You, my Lord. I
must let You carry
them for me. Most
of all, help me be
willing not to take
them back.

*W*hether I am
well-fed or hungry,
in plenty or want,
healthy or ill, I
know You will
guide me through
by Your strength.

*P*eace I leave with you. . . . I do not give to you as the world gives. Do not let your hearts be troubled and do not be afraid.

JOHN 14:27 NIV

$\mathscr{A}$t times like this, Lord, I can hardly stand all the hurts, tragedies, and sin in this world. Lord, please take me Home. I'm tired of being here.

I read in Your Word when You said, "Not My will, but Thine be done." If you need to keep me here, so be it, dear Lord, although I long to be with You.

$\mathcal{G}$ ive ear, O Lord, unto my prayer; and attend to the voice of my supplications.

In the day of my trouble I will call upon thee; for thou wilt answer me.

PSALM 86:6–7 KJV

Father, I am broken. I have nothing to offer You but pieces of my life. Pick them up, I pray, and use them.

*T*hank You for the miracle You create from my shattered life. Thank You for how You are making me into a beautiful new vessel to be used for You.

*T*he Lord is nigh unto them that are of a broken heart; and saveth such as be of a contrite spirit.

PSALM 34:18 KJV

$\mathcal{L}$ ord, I let myself get caught up in doing too many things. Bitterness and resentment are creeping in. Forgive me, Lord, and heal me.

*R*enew my strength, Lord, that I, too, can mount like the eagle. Please clip my wings just a little to keep me nearer to You, to learn my limitations.

$\mathcal{G}$ ive me the strength to say, "No thank you," in a loving, but firm way. Help me not to feel guilty. Perhaps I'm cheating others from the chance to serve.

G rant me wisdom in setting the right priorities: You first, my family second, and others next. Somewhere in there, show me how to take time for me.

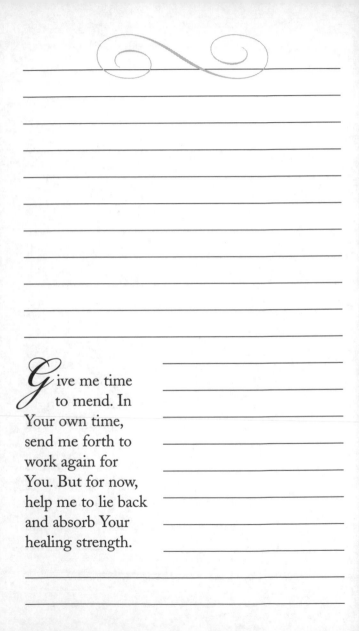

*G*ive me time to mend. In Your own time, send me forth to work again for You. But for now, help me to lie back and absorb Your healing strength.

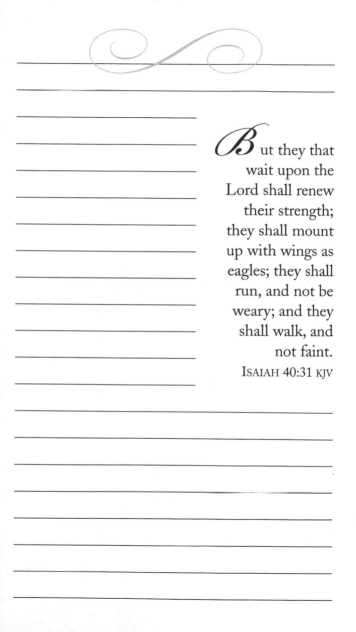

*B*ut they that wait upon the Lord shall renew their strength; they shall mount up with wings as eagles; they shall run, and not be weary; and they shall walk, and not faint.

ISAIAH 40:31 KJV

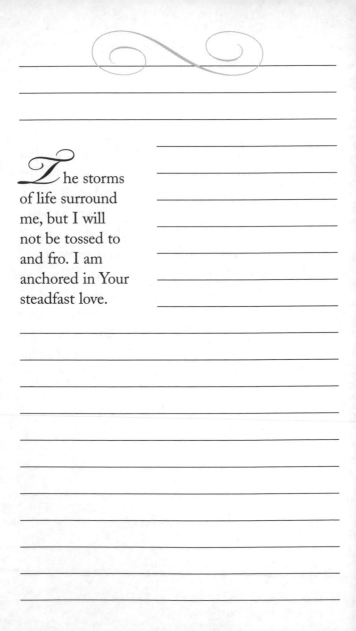

The storms of life surround me, but I will not be tossed to and fro. I am anchored in Your steadfast love.

I will call on Your name for peace. I will trust in You and will not feel afraid, as I nestle into Your protecting hands.

*E*ven now, I
hear Your whisper,
"Peace, be still.
Know I am
Your God."

*A*nd he arose and rebuked the wind, and said unto the sea, Peace, be still. And the wind ceased, and there was a great calm.

MARK 4:39–40 KJV

$\mathcal{D}$ear Father,
I pray You will
help me with my
job. Things aren't
going right. I
dread going to
work, and I need
Your direction.

*W*hen I do menial tasks, help me remember when Your Son, though King of Kings, came down from heaven and often acted as a servant.

I know I can earn my pay and make a living; or I can give of myself and make a life.

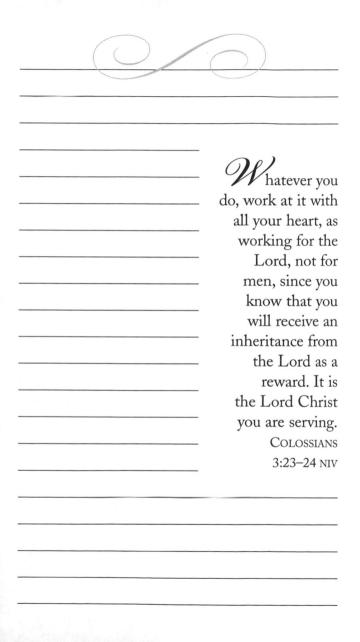

*W*hatever you
do, work at it with
all your heart, as
working for the
Lord, not for
men, since you
know that you
will receive an
inheritance from
the Lord as a
reward. It is
the Lord Christ
you are serving.
COLOSSIANS
3:23–24 NIV

You promised
You would
never leave or for-
sake me. I know
You are holding
my hand each day,
gently leading me
through the good
times and the bad.

O Lord, nothing can separate me from Your love. Not death, not life. Surely not the angels. Even the powers of hell cannot keep Your love from me.

$\mathcal{T}$oday's fears
and tomorrow's
worries are need-
less in light of
Your divine love.

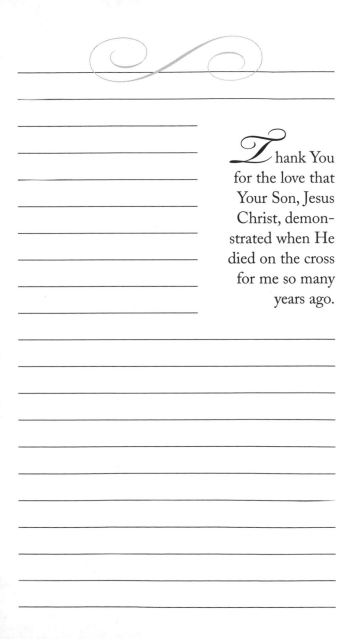

*T*hank You for the love that Your Son, Jesus Christ, demonstrated when He died on the cross for me so many years ago.

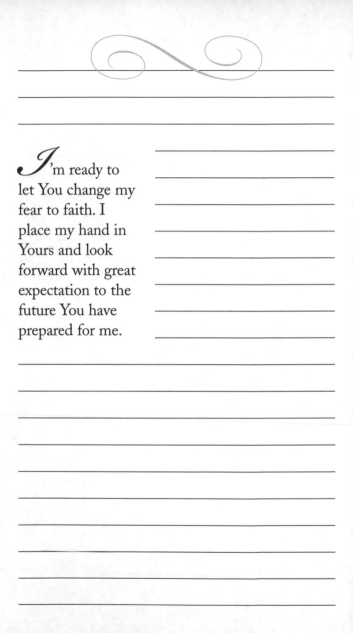

$\mathcal{I}$'m ready to
let You change my
fear to faith. I
place my hand in
Yours and look
forward with great
expectation to the
future You have
prepared for me.

*A*nd we know that all things work together for good to them that love God, to them who are the called according to his purpose.

ROMANS 8:28 KJV

I am always
watching over you,
no matter where
you are or how
difficult times
may be for you.
There is no limit
to My power as
I help you."

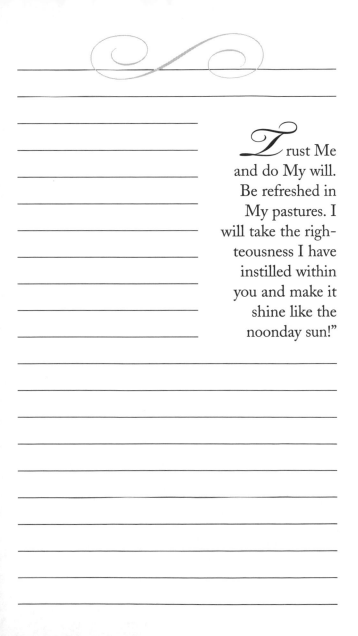

Trust Me
and do My will.
Be refreshed in
My pastures. I
will take the righ-
teousness I have
instilled within
you and make it
shine like the
noonday sun!"

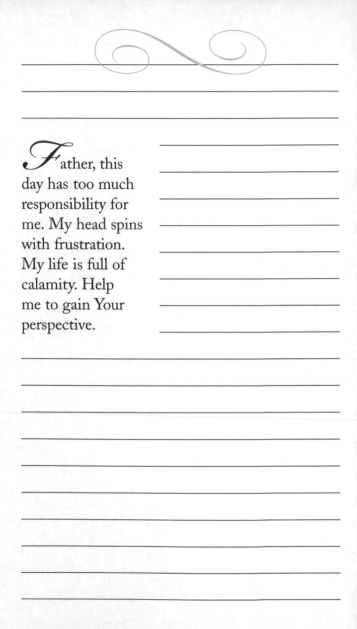

$\mathcal{F}$ather, this day has too much responsibility for me. My head spins with frustration. My life is full of calamity. Help me to gain Your perspective.

*W*hen I am weak, lend me Your quiet, confident strength; when impatient, grant me Your patience.

$\mathcal{K}$eep my
steps close
behind—not in
front of—You and
protect me with
Your strong hands.

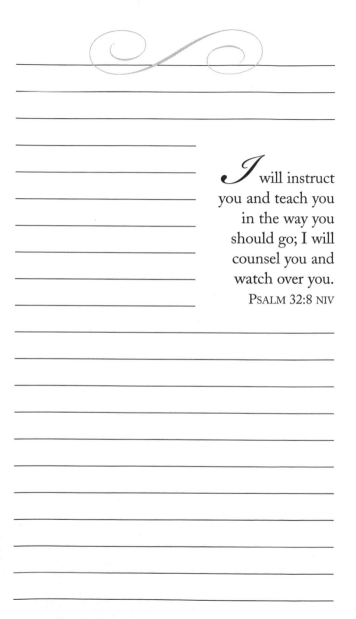

I will instruct
you and teach you
in the way you
should go; I will
counsel you and
watch over you.
PSALM 32:8 NIV

$\mathcal{I}$t's easy in our fast-paced world to let life control our schedules. We need to pull off life's fast lane for awhile and turn to God for direction and strength.

Let's tune in to His voice and marvel as He prepares the way for us. As we seek His direction, He miraculously makes more time in our day. Then at night we can look back and be satisfied within His will.

. . *b* ut as for me and my household, we will serve the Lord.
JOSHUA 24:15 NIV

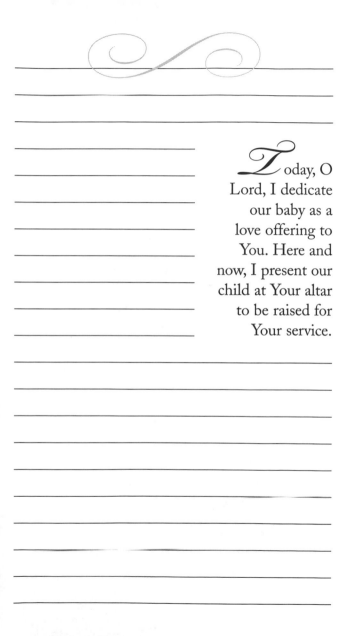

*T*oday, O Lord, I dedicate our baby as a love offering to You. Here and now, I present our child at Your altar to be raised for Your service.

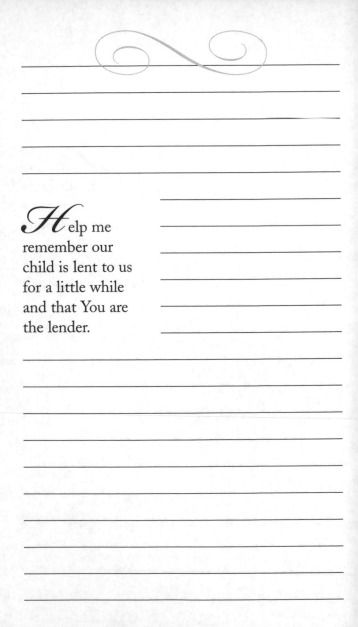

*H*elp me
remember our
child is lent to us
for a little while
and that You are
the lender.

The Lord
bless you and keep
you; the Lord
make his face
shine upon you
and be gracious
to you; the Lord
turn his face
toward you and
give you peace.
NUMBERS 6:24–26 NIV

*W*ill I live to see my children grown? Will I live to see my grandchildren? My great-grandchildren? I can only trust and make each day count for something.

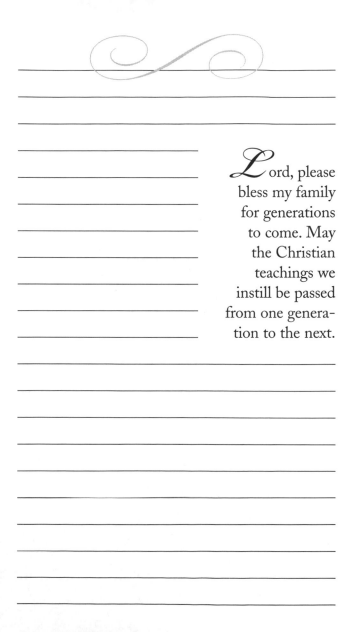

*L*ord, please
bless my family
for generations
to come. May
the Christian
teachings we
instill be passed
from one genera-
tion to the next.

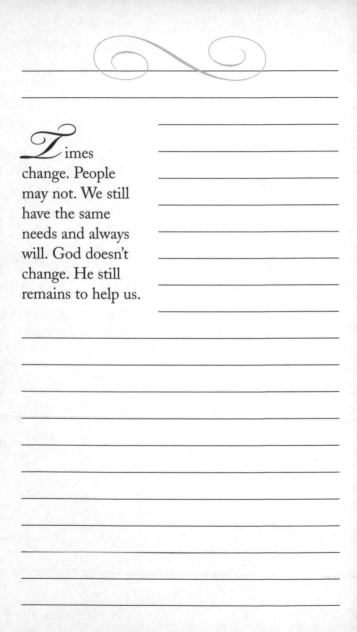

$\mathcal{T}$imes change. People may not. We still have the same needs and always will. God doesn't change. He still remains to help us.

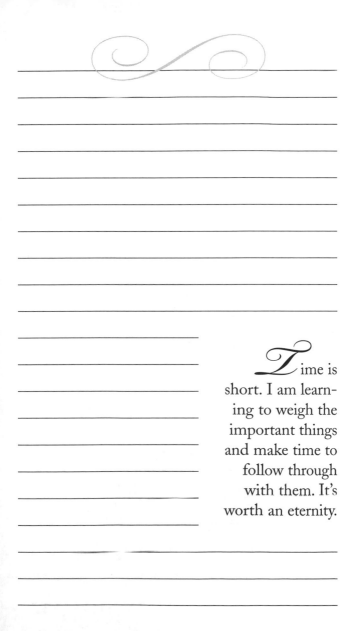

$\mathcal{T}$ime is short. I am learning to weigh the important things and make time to follow through with them. It's worth an eternity.

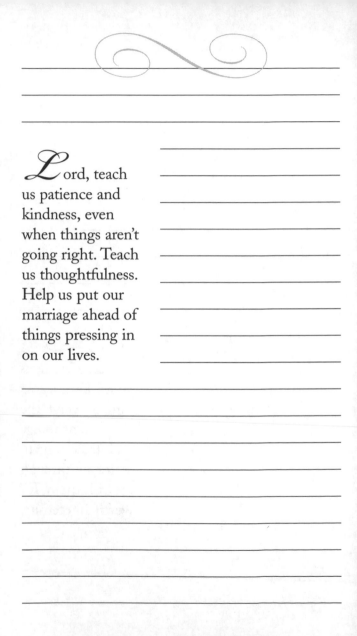

*L*ord, teach us patience and kindness, even when things aren't going right. Teach us thoughtfulness. Help us put our marriage ahead of things pressing in on our lives.

$\mathcal{L}$et us be
willingly inconve-
nienced for one
another's needs
and quick to go
the second mile,
then the third.

*I*n our hurried
schedules, let
us look for time
to spend with
each other.

$\mathcal{W}$e have fallen in love with each other over and over again, even while changing.

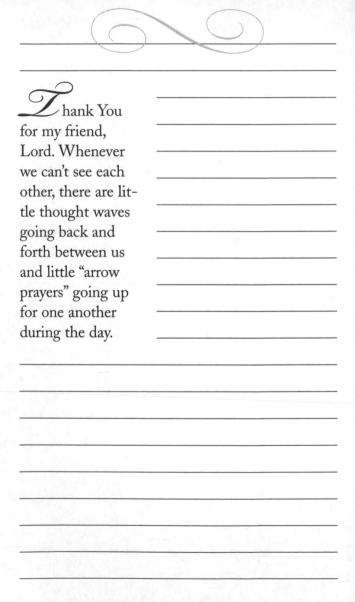

$\mathcal{T}$hank You
for my friend,
Lord. Whenever
we can't see each
other, there are lit-
tle thought waves
going back and
forth between us
and little "arrow
prayers" going up
for one another
during the day.

*H*elp me never to take my friend for granted but to treat her with thoughtfulness. Help me to recognize when she wants my company and when she needs time alone.

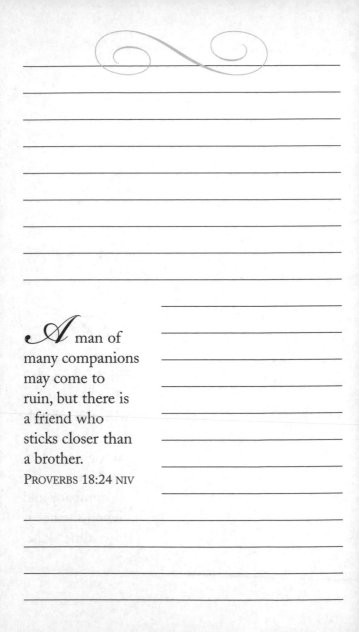

A man of
many companions
may come to
ruin, but there is
a friend who
sticks closer than
a brother.
PROVERBS 18:24 NIV

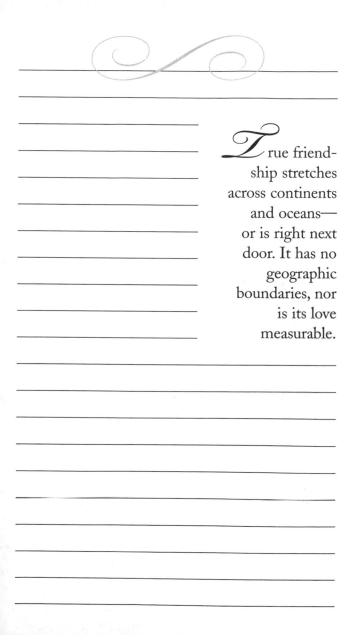

True friendship stretches across continents and oceans— or is right next door. It has no geographic boundaries, nor is its love measurable.

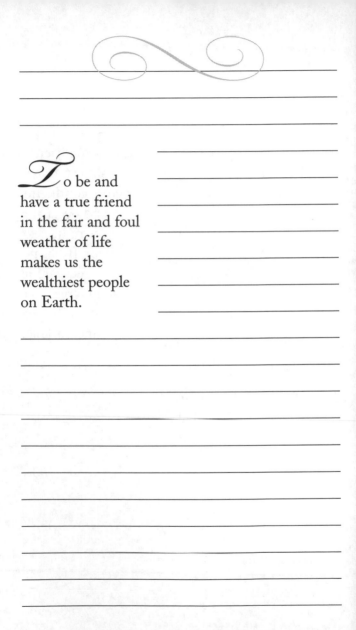

To be and have a true friend in the fair and foul weather of life makes us the wealthiest people on Earth.

*T*houghtful notes, phone calls, and selfless actions create warm, happy memories that last a lifetime.

I will sing of the mercies of the Lord for ever: with my mouth will I make known thy faithfulness to all generations.

PSALM 89:1 KJV

I look at the trees; their roots sink deep by the stream. In the same way, let my roots sink deep into You.

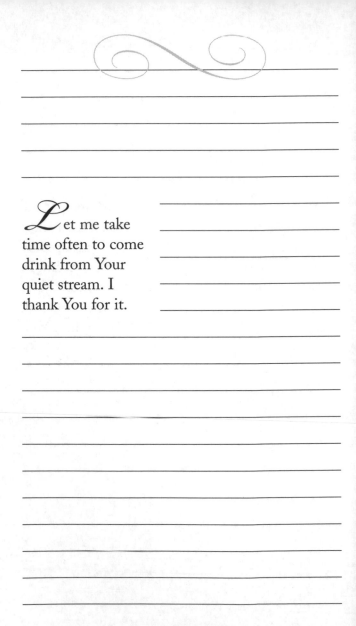

*L*et me take time often to come drink from Your quiet stream. I thank You for it.

The Lord is my shepherd I shall not want. He maketh me to lie down in green pastures: he leadeth me beside the still waters. He restoreth my soul.

PSALM 23:1–3 KJV

$\mathcal{L}$ord, I want
to praise You from
the pits. Not the
pits of self-pity,
but the pits
carefully placed in
the heart of love's
race track.

*S*trengthen my arms, I pray. Keep my feet swift and sure. Make each day's path level before me. With all my being, I run this race for You.

*W*hether
I'm weary or not,
in season or out,
I must begin
moving my
mountain, even
if it's only a tea-
spoonful at a time.

I trust You, for this mountain shall be removed, and I praise You for the victories to come.

*J*esus looked at
them and said,
"With man this
is impossible,
but with God
all things are
possible."
MATTHEW 19:26 NIV

*W*ouldn't it be wonderful if we could call on God and He would snap His fingers and make all our troubles disappear? It rarely works that way.

$\mathcal{T}$here are reasons God lets us struggle. There are lessons to learn and lives to touch along the way. At times our mountains prepare us to help others.

God is working
when another
dear one picks up
a teaspoon and
pitches in.

*T*he day comes when we look back at what we have accomplished with God's help in moving that mountain and carrying our cross.

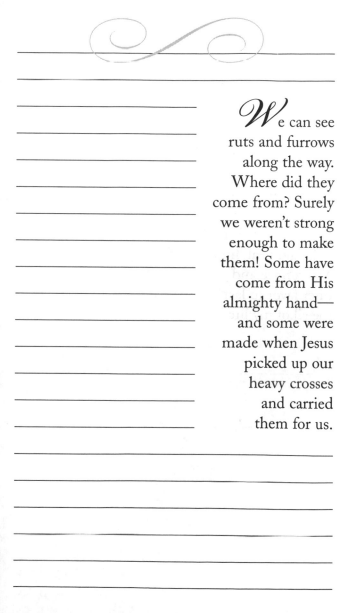

We can see ruts and furrows along the way. Where did they come from? Surely we weren't strong enough to make them! Some have come from His almighty hand—and some were made when Jesus picked up our heavy crosses and carried them for us.

$\mathscr{I}$ thank You, already, for how You lift me from the depths of despair, how You help and heal, how You forgive and offer favor to last me all of my life.

I will always
be secure in your
protection. I
won't be shaken.
I will stand stead-
fast and sure.
I will never give up.

I press on toward the goal to win the prize for which God has called me heavenward in Christ Jesus.

PHILIPPIANS 3:14 NIV

I know not what each day holds, or what time I have left to serve. This I do know, dear Lord, I want to leave my mark for You.

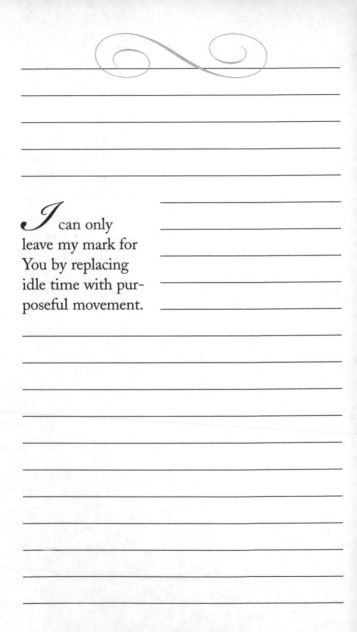

I can only leave my mark for You by replacing idle time with purposeful movement.

$\mathcal{T}$each me to
let go of yesterday,
live fully today,
and look with
excitement toward
tomorrow.

$\mathcal{M}$ ake a
joyful noise unto
the Lord, all ye
lands. Serve the
Lord with
gladness; come
before his presence
with singing.
PSALM 100:1–2 KJV

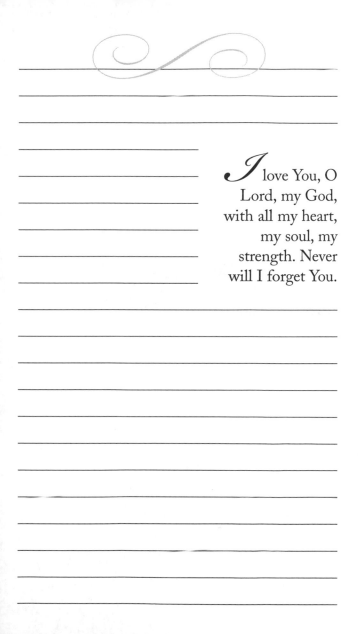

I love You, O Lord, my God, with all my heart, my soul, my strength. Never will I forget You.

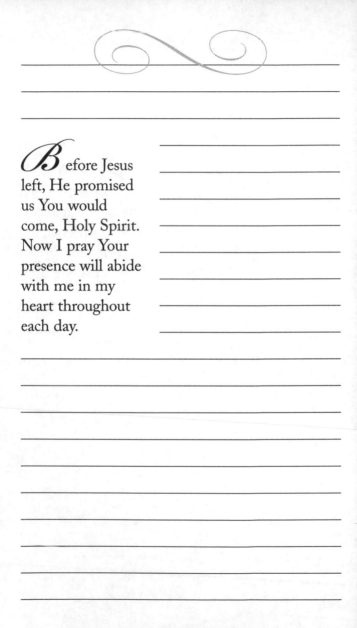

$\mathcal{B}$ efore Jesus left, He promised us You would come, Holy Spirit. Now I pray Your presence will abide with me in my heart throughout each day.

I cannot see
You, but I know
Your presence:
Your soft whispers,
Your warnings,
Your nudges,
Your warm,
steadfast love.

The grace
of the Lord Jesus
Christ, and love
of God, and the
communion of
the Holy Ghost,
be with you
all. Amen.
2 CORINTHIANS
13:14 KJV

*T*hank You for my church, these loving people, the body of Christ. And thank You for quieting my heart so I may listen to You.

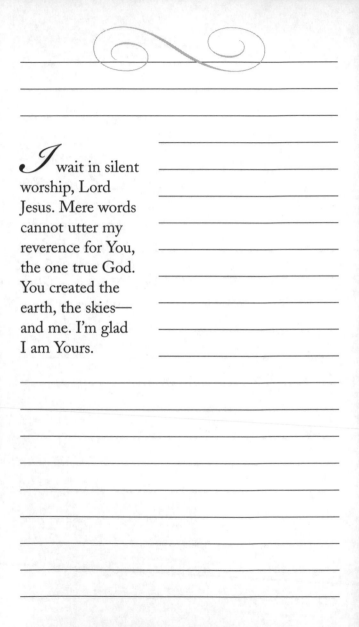

I wait in silent worship, Lord Jesus. Mere words cannot utter my reverence for You, the one true God. You created the earth, the skies—and me. I'm glad I am Yours.

$\mathcal{B}$e still," I
hear Him softly
say. "Be still,
lay all aside."

*F*ather, I offer
You my sacrifice
of praise. Forever
will I honor
Your name.

*N*o other is so worthy of my praise. You are power, wisdom, honor, glory, might, and blessing.

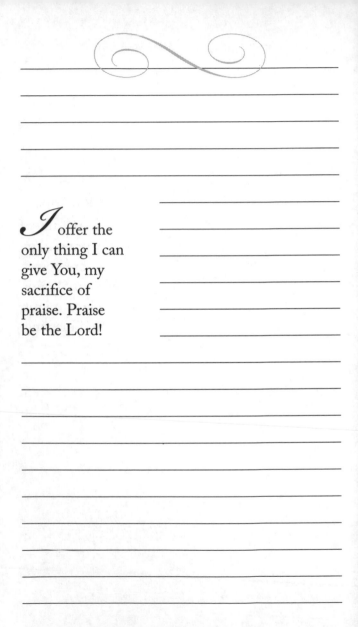

$\mathcal{I}$ offer the only thing I can give You, my sacrifice of praise. Praise be the Lord!

I will sacrifice
a thank offering to
you and call on the
name of the Lord.

PSALM 116:17 NIV

I lift my eyes to You, O Lord, my joy and strength. My heart quickens. New energy surges through my body. Gladness fills my heart as I concentrate on You.

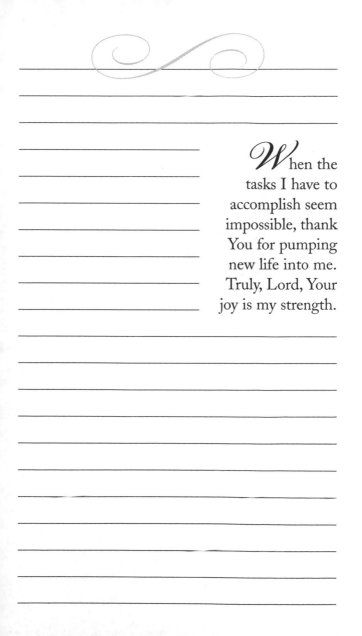

*W*hen the tasks I have to accomplish seem impossible, thank You for pumping new life into me. Truly, Lord, Your joy is my strength.

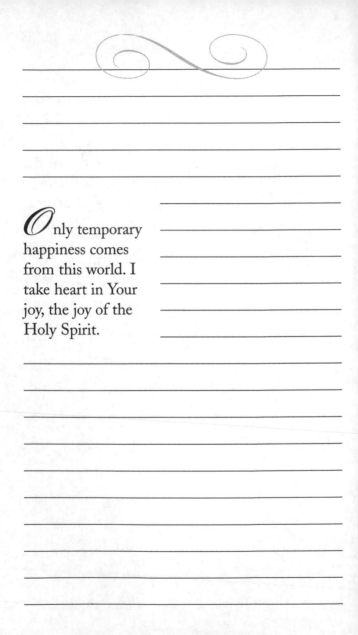

*O*nly temporary happiness comes from this world. I take heart in Your joy, the joy of the Holy Spirit.

*Y*our joy covers suffering, trials, sadness, and exhaustion. When I experience it, my cup overflows.

*Y*ou wipe away my tears and replace them with gladness anew and Your pure, sweet joy.

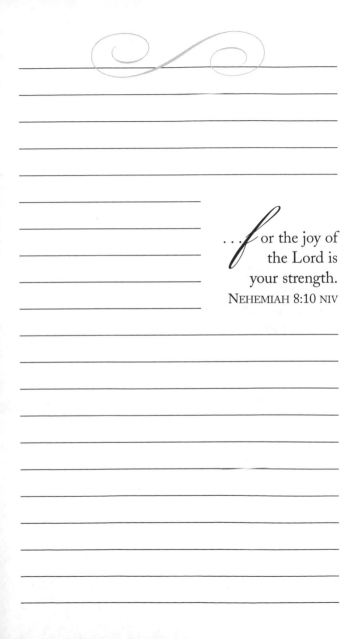

. . .*f*or the joy of
the Lord is
your strength.
NEHEMIAH 8:10 NIV

*J*esus, the words You uttered from the cross are so priceless. Thank You for keeping those promises true down through history, even to today.

*J*esus said,
"Father,
forgive them,
for they do not
know what they
are doing."
LUKE 23:33–34 NIV

*Thank You
for forgiveness.*

*J*esus answered
    him "I tell you
the truth, today
you will be with
me in paradise."
LUKE 23:42–43 NIV

*Thank You
for Paradise.*

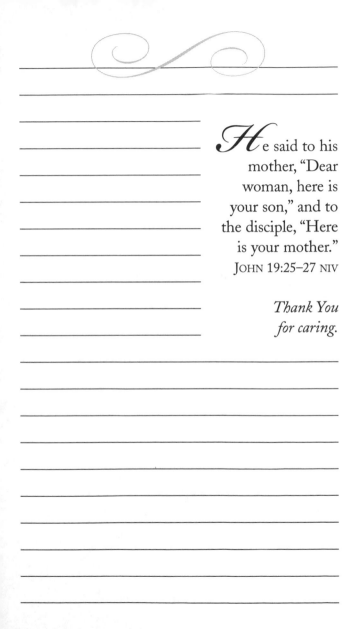

*H*e said to his
mother, "Dear
woman, here is
your son," and to
the disciple, "Here
is your mother."
JOHN 19:25–27 NIV

*Thank You
for caring.*

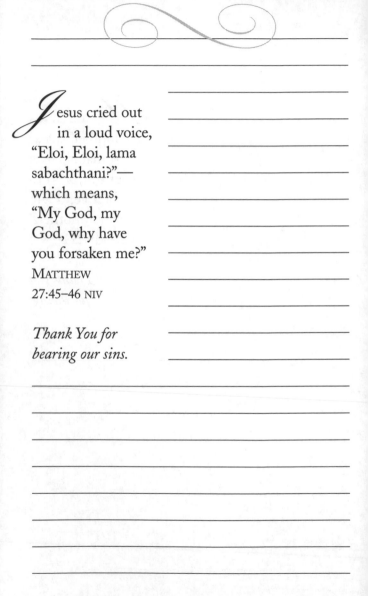

*J*esus cried out in a loud voice, "Eloi, Eloi, lama sabachthani?"— which means, "My God, my God, why have you forsaken me?"
MATTHEW 27:45–46 NIV

Thank You for bearing our sins.

*S*o that the
Scripture would
be fulfilled, Jesus
said, "I am thirsty."
JOHN 19:28 NIV

*Thank You for
living water.*

*W*hen he had received the drink, Jesus said, "It is finished." With that, he bowed his head and gave up his spirit.
JOHN 19:30 NIV

Thank You for fulfilling God's promise to save us.

_J_esus called out
with a loud voice,
"Father, into your
hands I commit
my spirit."
LUKE 23:46 NIV

*Thank You
for victory!*

*W*hen troubles surround me, Lord, I will trust in You. I hide within Your cloak of safety.

*W*hen all seems impossible, You are my mighty Deliverer. Even though I am unworthy, You perform marvelous wonders in my life.

*A*lone, I amount to nothing. As I obey and serve You, others can see Your wondrous works within me.

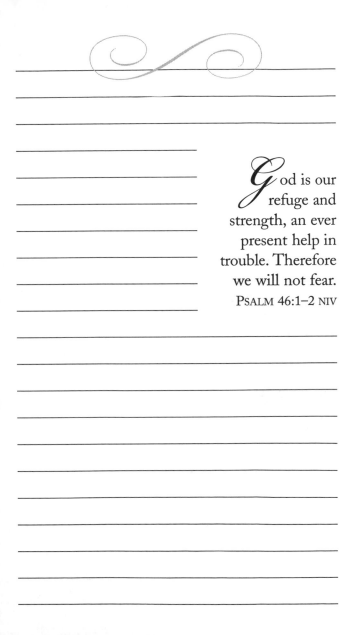

*G*od is our
refuge and
strength, an ever
present help in
trouble. Therefore
we will not fear.
PSALM 46:1–2 NIV

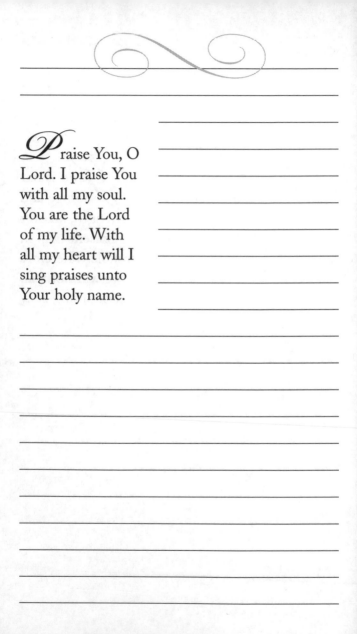

*P*raise You, O Lord. I praise You with all my soul. You are the Lord of my life. With all my heart will I sing praises unto Your holy name.

My hope is in You, my God, my help and strength. You who created the heaven, the earth, the sea, are everything.

I shall not put my confidence in people of high places, nor in any mortal. They can't grant me life eternal. Only You can, Lord.

*H*ow good it is to sing praises to our God, how pleasant and fitting to praise him!

PSALM 147:1 NIV

*Y*ou, dear Father, are my Rock and my Defender; I shall not fear. I know in whom I believe, and I'm persuaded You keep me close to You day by day.

Thou wilt keep him in perfect peace, whose mind is stayed on thee: because he trusteth in thee.

ISAIAH 26:3 KJV

I love You,
Lord. Even
though I have
never seen You, I
still believe in You.
I love You because
I know You first
loved me.

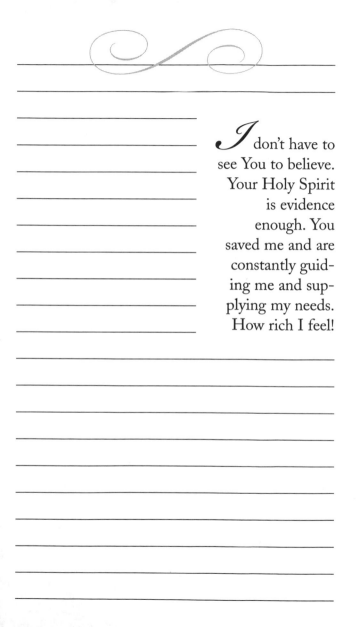

$\mathcal{I}$ don't have to see You to believe. Your Holy Spirit is evidence enough. You saved me and are constantly guiding me and supplying my needs. How rich I feel!

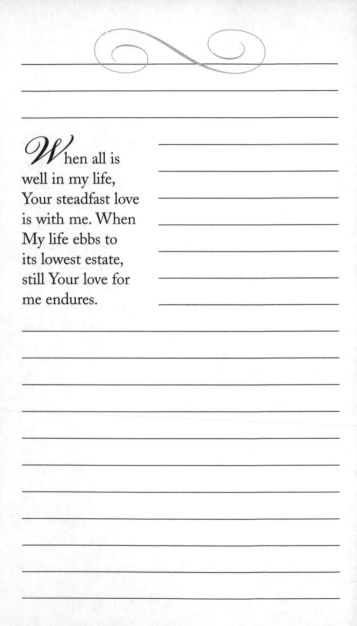

*W*hen all is well in my life, Your steadfast love is with me. When My life ebbs to its lowest estate, still Your love for me endures.

When my enemies threaten me, You surround me with Your protection. You provide me with food and clothing. How grateful I am.

I praise You, Lord, for the beauty You loaned me on this earth. Although I'll only be here a short time, I pray for Your wisdom so I may responsibly care for this earth.

The earth is
the Lord's and
everything in it,
the world, and all
who live in it.
PSALM 24:1 NIV

$\mathcal{B}$ ecause of
Your forgiving
grace, I'm learning
to forgive.

*Y*our endless
love over-
flows like an
artesian well.
Because of this,
I pass it on
to others.

*W*ith an eager mind and bending will, I await direction from You. I long to serve You in word and deed.

*I*n my car, on the bus, in the elevator, on my job, in a meeting, in the kitchen, even at a ball game, I will keep my heart tuned and bless You.

*T*hank You, Father, for always being with me, not only now but for eternity.

You ou remain the same yesterday, today, and through all the tomorrows to come.

*E*ven though
You never change,
You perceive every
season of my life.

*T*hank You,
Lord, for taking
time to know
everything about
me and for
caring for my
insignificant
(yet important
to me) needs.

*E*verything that is good and perfect comes from You, O Lord and Creator. You shine on my life day and night with no shadow of turning away.

*T*hank You for keeping the promises You gave in Your word. You never forsake, You never fail. You are truth, You are life.

$\mathcal{W}$hat a comfort to know You will live forever and ever, and that I can always be with You.

*B*ut I trusted
in thee, O Lord: I
said, Thou art my
God. My times are
in thy hand.
PSALM 31:14–15 KJV

Inspirational Library

Beautiful purse/pocket-size editions of Christian classics bound in flexible leatherette. These books make thoughtful gifts for everyone on your list, including yourself!

When I'm on My Knees   The highly popular collection of devotional thoughts on prayer, especially for women.
Flexible Leatherette $4.97

The Bible Promise Book   Over 1,000 promises from God's Word arranged by topic. What does God promise about matters like: Anger, Illness, Jealousy, Love, Money, Old Age, and Mercy? Find out in this book!
Flexible Leatherette $3.97

Daily Wisdom for Women   A daily devotional for women seeking biblical wisdom to apply to their lives. Scripture taken from the New American Standard Version of the Bible.
Flexible Leatherette $4.97

My Daily Prayer Journal   Each page is dated and features a Scripture verse and ample room for you to record your thoughts, prayers, and praises. One page for each day of the year.
Flexible Leatherette $4.97

Available wherever books are sold.
Or order from:

Barbour Publishing, Inc.
P.O. Box 719
Uhrichsville, OH 44683
http://www.barbourbooks.com

If you order by mail, add $2.00 to your order for shipping.
Prices are subject to change without notice.